ISBN 978-1-330-77297-3
PIBN 10103536

For support please visit www.forgottenbooks.com

English
Français
Deutsche
Italiano
Español
Português

www.forgottenbooks.com

Mythology Photography **Fiction**
Fishing Christianity **Art** Cooking
Essays Buddhism Freemasonry
Medicine **Biology** Music **Ancient
Egypt** Evolution Carpentry Physics
Dance Geology **Mathematics** Fitness
Shakespeare **Folklore** Yoga Marketing
Confidence Immortality Biographies
Poetry **Psychology** Witchcraft
Electronics Chemistry History **Law**
Accounting **Philosophy** Anthropology
Alchemy Drama Quantum Mechanics
Atheism Sexual Health **Ancient History**
Entrepreneurship Languages Sport
Paleontology Needlework Islam
Metaphysics Investment Archaeology
Parenting Statistics Criminology
Motivational

The
Peril of Prussianism

By

Douglas Wilson Johnson
**Associate Professor of Physiography in
Columbia University**

G. P. Putnam's Sons
New York and London
The ·Knickerbocker Press
1917

D
515
J65

659305

16. 5. 57

The Knickerbocker Press, New York

FOREWORD

THE following pages contain the substance of an address delivered by the writer before the annual convention of the Iowa Bankers Association at Des Moines on June 14, 1917. A request from the bankers of one section of the State that the address be printed in German for circulation among the large German-born population of their district, together with a number of enquiries for copies of the English text, have tempted me to believe that some good purpose might be served by publishing the address in its present form.

However opinions may have differed in the past as to our duty in the world crisis, there can be no two opinions regarding our duty to-day. America has decided that splendid isolation is no longer possible in a world rendered wondrous small by the swift steamship and express train, the telegraph and telephone, the cable and wireless telegraphy. We *are* our brothers' keeper, and have entered on a policy of international co-operation, first to compel a just peace, and then to preserve it undisturbed from future assaults by autocratic militarism. We have pledged our faith and must fight a good fight to make the world safe for democracy. Every ounce of the national strength must be brought to bear, every man in the whole country must render loyal, devoted service. The Stars and Stripes have never yet been unfurled in a lost cause. They must not now go down to defeat.

The only assurance of success lies in the unswerving devotion of our whole people to a cause they believe sacred. It is imperative therefore that the issues of the present war be made clear to every citizen. Americans will not support with enthusiasm a cause they do not understand, nor shed their blood with unmeasured generosity to achieve ends they cannot see. If the following pages help a few among my fellow-citizens to measure the magnitude of the cause we serve, they will not have been written in vain.

DOUGLAS W. JOHNSON.

NEW YORK, July 1, 1917.

CONTENTS

vii

The Peril of Prussianism

I

TWO IDEALS OF GOVERNMENT

THERE exist in the world two fundamentally opposed ideals of government. One is based on the conception that the government is the servant of its citizens and exists for their benefit. According to this conception the divine right of the individual to life, liberty, and the pursuit of happiness must be conserved, and the most successful government is the one which most effectively promotes the free development of its citizens. The growth of this ideal of government can be traced through the whole history of the Anglo-Saxon race, but first reached its full fruition in the American Declaration of Independence. Because of the supreme faith of our forefathers in dedicating their lives, their fortunes, and their sacred honor to the maintenance of this ideal in the New World, Canada and the other English colonies to-day enjoy a freedom which would not otherwise be theirs. The loss of her American colonies taught England the fearful cost of obstructing man's aspirations for true self-government, with the result that both in her colonies and at home the growth of democratic ideals has seldom been seriously checked. France lit her torch of freedom at the American altar, and in Russia when the bureaucrats would denounce Milyukof for his democratic aspirations they hurl at him the epithet "American." It

No. 1.

will not appear unseemly, therefore, to call the ideal of government just described "The American ideal." In a peculiar degree America has long stood before the world as its champion and defender.

The second ideal of government is diametrically opposed to the first. It is based on the conception that the individual is the servant of the government and exists for the benefit of the government. According to this ideal, the State is everything, the individual nothing. The perfect government is one which so disciplines its citizens that they render absolute and unquestioning obedience to every order of the State, performing with machine-like precision the tasks assigned to them. Organized efficiency and team work replace the uncoördinated and ineffectual efforts of individuals which forever clog the clumsy mechanism of democracy. Individual liberty is per-

mitted only where it does not interfere
with the good of the State, and it is the
State, not the citizen, which decides
where the line shall be drawn. This
ideal of government was more than once
introduced into England, but has never
seemed to thrive among Anglo-Saxon
peoples. France suffered it for a space,
then permanently rejected it. Russia
endured it with ever increasing protest,
and after long years of bitter struggle and
threatening revolution has at last tram-
pled it under foot. But among Teutonic
peoples it has thriven amazingly. Its
supreme development is bound up with
the history of Prussia, and reaches its
most perfect manifestation in the modern
state of Prussianized Germany. As Professor Münsterberg has truly said, "In
the German view the State is not for the
individuals, but the individuals for the
State." Both Kaiser and people unite

in presenting to the world the most efficient example of a government paternally solicitous for the material welfare of its citizens, docilely served by a disciplined people rendering unquestioning obedience to the commands of their sovereign. Assuredly this second ideal of government is preëminently the Prussian ideal.

II

THE INESCAPABLE CONFLICT

HAVING placed in contrast the American ideal and the Prussian ideal of government, let us next consider this all-important fact: *The two ideals are mutually antagonistic, and cannot long exist in the world side by side.* This statement may on first thought seem extreme. One may ask, "Cannot every nation select that one of the two ideals of government which it prefers, leaving every other nation in peace to do the same? Is there not room enough in the world for the peaceful development of both ideals?" The answer is in the negative, and for this reason: The Prussian ideal denies one of the primitive instincts of mankind, the instinct of individual freedom and personal sovereignty. From the beginning, man has rebelled against slavery, whether the enslaving power be beneficent or brutal. An inefficient government of his own creation is more tolerable to him than the most efficient control imposed by another. A people enjoying unwonted prosperity may for a time docilely submit to the hand which feeds them; but sooner or later the instinct of freedom will assert itself and the people grow restless. Especially is this true where the people enslaved by an autocratic government are surrounded by freemen who govern themselves. Liberty is an inevitable, unconscious proselyter.

There remains to the autocratic government but one procedure. It must offer to its subjects compensation for their slavery, and destroy the proselyting influence which surrounds them. Both are accomplished at one stroke by military conquest. Just as freemen will undergo stern military discipline for the sake of victory, so a subject people will submit to a ruler who assures them military glory and the privilege of triumphing over their neighbors. Autocracy and aggressive militarism are inextricably bound together. Through militarism autocracy must conquer the world, or from a peaceful penetration of the ideals of liberty it will suffer decay.

No one understands this truth more clearly than does the autocratic government of Germany. Its motto, "World power or downfall," is not the silly ranting of a wild extremist, but a brutally frank statement of a profound truth. The German government's oft-repeated assertion that it is fighting a defensive warfare should not be pushed aside as an idle falsehood. The tide of popular discontent with autocracy was beginning to rise in Germany, and the autocratic government's most effective defence was a war which should unite the people once more in loyal subjection. Prior to July, 1914, the German papers were publicly ridiculing the Kaiser's pompous assertion of his divine right to rule, and were indignantly denouncing his angry threat to tear the Constitution of Alsace in shreds and annex the unhappy province to Prussia; representatives of the people in increasing numbers were refusing to vote the government's burdensome war taxes and were protesting against the exaltation of military above civil authority. A month later, the entire nation was enthusiastically acclaiming the war lord whose victorious legions were sweeping across Belgium to carry German dominion to the shores of the English Channel. Never was the Hohenzollern dynasty more securely in the saddle than during the many months when flag-bedecked Germany was celebrating her victories on every front. An offensive warfare against Germany's neighbors had proven the best defensive warfare for Germany's government.

The Hohenzollern kingdom of Prussia in 1740, when Frederick the Great ascended the throne. The scat domains extend from the Rhine eastward beyond the Vistula.

III

GROWTH OF PRUSSIANISM

THE historical development of the Prussian ideal of government shows Prussia's realization of the fact that nothing save the most aggressive exploitation of that ideal would prevent its ultimate extinction. Some time before the discovery of America by Columbus, there appeared on the world stage an unimportant house by the name of Hohenzollern which ruled over a small tract of country surrounding the little town of Berlin (see map, Figure 1). Successive rulers of this line added to their holdings by conquering neighboring lands, until the scattered domains under Prussian control stretched from the banks of the Rhine eastward beyond the Vistula. In 1640, there came to the throne one of the most famous among the early exponents of the Prussian ideal of government, Frederick William, the Great Elector. He is described as "coarse by nature, heartless in destroying opponents, treacherous in diplomatic negotiations, and entirely devoid of refinement." Fully realizing that the Prussian theory of government could live only by perpetuating and extending the policy of conquest successfully pursued by his Hohenzollern ancestors, he organized, against the protests of his subjects, an enormous standing army, the beginning of the modern Prussian military machine.

. It would not be profitable to trace in detail the particular part played by each Hohenzollern ruler in exploiting the Prussian ideal of government. It is the

proud boast of the Hohenzollern dynasty
that almost every one of its members has
in peace or in war added something to
the extent of Prussian dominions. The
rough and boorish Frederick William I.
scoured all Europe in search of tall men
for his armies, selling the royal jewels
and turning the family table silver into
money to defray the cost of building up
an invincible military machine for further
conquest. His son and successor dis-
liked military pursuits, preferring the
company of music and books. But he,
too, realized on ascending the throne that
the Prussian ideal of government could
not endure apart from a policy of aggressive militarism, and skillfully employing
the military machine painstakingly per-
fected by his thrifty father, he became
the all-powerful Frederick the Great, one
of the most renowned military geniuses
of history. Silesia was brutally wrenched

from the helpless young Empress of Austria without the pretense of an excuse, and the shameful partition of Poland was successfully begun. Militarism approximately doubled the size of Prussia in the lifetime of this one man (see Figures 2 and 3).

The time soon came when the normal growth of the Prussian ideal of government demanded the extension of Prussian influence on an enormous scale. Thus far the Hohenzollern dominion had risen by successive acquisitions from a small province surrounding Berlin to a European power (Figure 4). It must next ascend to the position of a world power. To accomplish this two things were essential. Austria had long been a powerful rival of Prussia in the struggle for dominant influence among the smaller German states. Since the absorption of Austria was not yet possible, her influence

must be destroyed by military defeat.
With Austria eliminated, Prussian domination over the remaining German states
must be consolidated, to the end that a
great Germanic power, pledged to the
support of Hohenzollernism and the
Prussian ideal of government, should
arise in the world.   Two remarkable men
undertook this colossal task. William
I. of Prussia, grandfather of the present
Kaiser, bent all his energies to developing
the military resources of his kingdom,
while Bismarck proceeded to apply his
policy of blood and iron.   In defiance of
the Prussian parliament which refused to
vote taxes for a great army, in defiance
of the constitution which guaranteed
to the parliament control over taxes, and
in defiance of the voice of the people as
expressed in the public press, the military
machine was enormously strengthened.
William I. and the Iron Chancellor knew

that all crimes against the people's liberty would be forgotten when a war of conquest had been successfully concluded.

In the course of a few months, the Danish provinces of Schleswig and Holstein were conquered and annexed to Prussia, Austria was overwhelmingly defeated and her influence destroyed, and a number of the independent north German states which sided with Austria were brought under Prussian control. Soon after, the south German states were brought into the Prussian union for a new war of conquest, Alsace-Lorraine and a huge indemnity were extracted from prostrate France, and the Hohenzollern king of Prussia became the autocratic ruler of a great world power, the modern German Empire (Figure 5). The Prussian ideal of government was now firmly established among a great people pledged to a policy of aggressive militarism.

It is well for us to review these salient facts of Prussian history, lest we forget that from the earliest time the house of Hohenzollern has efficiently and consistently pursued a single policy which inevitably involves the maintenance of a great military machine and the periodic employment of that machine in ever-enlarging conquests of neighboring territory. He is blind indeed who would imagine that, after pursuing a given policy for five hundred years with phenomenal success, the Prussian Government should to-day suddenly abandon that policy in favor of another which it truthfully admits would lead to the downfall of a painstakingly reared autocracy. Both the nature of the Prussian ideal of government and the facts of Prussian history assure us that Germany is to-day,

as she has ever been in the past, strug-
gling for world domination in order to
prevent the downfall of the autocratic
Hohenzollern rule.

Prussia in 1786, at the death of Frederick the Great. Silesia has been forcibly wrested from Austria, and the seizure of Polish territory accomplished.

2

IV

THE MAILED FIST AT WORK

FORTUNATELY for our clearness of vision, Germany's plans for her next step toward the goal of world domination are too plain to be doubted. They are precisely what Prussian history would lead us to expect. A petty Hohenzollern province first dominates Prussia, Prussia then dominates Germany, and now the plans provide that Germany shall dominate Europe. The method of achieving the desired end is precisely the same with which history has made us so familiar. Adjacent territories are to be brought under Hohenzollern rule by the annexation of some and the federation of others into a great Central European Empire, with Germany' the directing force and the Prussian military machine the invincible bond which holds them together. Let us lift the curtain for a moment and watch the mailed fist as it moves the pieces on the European chessboard in preparation for the coup of 1914.

We see the evil hand in Vienna, shaping the policy of the Dual Monarchy and gaining that ascendency over its affairs which has reduced Austria-Hungary to a state of vassalage. We observe Italy bound in unholy alliance with the historic enemy of Italian freedom. We realize that it is the mailed fist acting through Austria in the seizure of Bosnia and Herzegovina in flagrant violation of treaty pledges. We behold the Prussian war lord appear "in shining armor" beside his obedient Austrian vassal to threaten Russia when she protests against this

injury to her brother Slavs. We see
Servia robbed of her hard-won port on
the Adriatic and Albania erected into a
make-believe kingdom under Austrian
tutelage; and we recognize the old, familiar
methods of the Hohenzollern. We find
the mailed fist clasping in fraternal greet-
ing the bloody hand that massacres
the Armenians, the Emperor of Christian
Germany becoming a brother to the unspeakable Turk, training and officering
his armies, and securing from him con-
cessions for the future Berlin to Bagdad
railway. We see puppet Hohenzollern
kings placed on the thrones of Bulgaria
and Roumania, and King Constantine of
Greece married to the Kaiser's sister.
We watch the meshes of German intrigue
wound about the Russian Government,
and the mighty Slav reduced to partial
impotence. By ruthless conquest and by
peaceful penetration, the stage is being

set for the great Central European Empire, while at home the war lord prepares for the coming contest by accumulating military stores in quantities which have since astonished the world, by forcing the passage of a naval bill destined to make Germany formidable on sea as well as on land, by enlarging the Kiel Canal to permit the passage of the largest battleships, by building heavy-metalled, double-tracked railways along the borders of Belgium and other peaceful neighbors, by securing a grant of $250,-000,000 in special war taxes with which to raise the army to a peace footing of 700,000 men and a war footing of nearly ten millions, and by marshalling the voices of obedient professors and the pens of servile writers in one vast campaign of education, designed to poison the German mind with dreams of Pan-Germanic power.

At last the propitious moment is arrived, and the mailed fist pulls the strings. Austria approaches Italy with the proposition, that they unite in the conquest of Servia; but Italy refuses. A delay of some months ensues, while European diplomats struggle to avert the impending calamity. Then an Austrian prince is murdered in the capital city of conquered Bosnia. This furnishes the desired excuse for beginning the long-planned war. Vienna secretly confers with Berlin, and at the end of a month of silence suddenly astounds the civilized world by accusing the Servian Government of the murder, and submitting ten demands designed to be so humiliating in their nature and so insulting in their tone as to insure a prompt rejection. But unfortunately for the Hohenzollern plan Servia, on the advice of her peaceably inclined friends, accepts outright eight of the unjust demands and agrees to submit to arbitration the remaining two which seriously threaten her independence. This is most disconcerting, but the plan must not be balked. War is therefore declared on Servia despite her humiliating surrender, and the mobilization of Russia in support of Servia gives Berlin the pretext for declarations of war against Russia, France, and Belgium. The work of conquering and consolidating a great Central European Empire under Prussian control is now in full swing according to the most approved Hohenzollern methods.

V

A WOLF IN SHEEP'S CLOTHING

IT cannot be denied that as things stand to-day the plans for a Prussianized Central Europe have succeeded to a remarkable degree (see Figure 6). Austria has come wholly under German domination, and is dependent upon the Prussian military machine for her very existence. Without its help, Serbs and Russians are able to defeat her at will. Her armies are but tools in the hands of German higher officers, while her political administration is dominated by Berlin. Eager for peace to-day, she dares not ask for it till the Kaiser has given the word. Said an Austrian army officer, who had

25

fought through the Galician campaign: "Our worst enemy is not Russia but the Prussian Government. If the war is won by the Germans there will be no Austria." To an even greater degree Bulgaria and Turkey have become vassals of the Hohenzollern state, taking their orders direct from Berlin. German troops in Constantinople and German warships in the harbor hold the government of the Turk in abject servitude. The control of two thirds of Roumania has passed into German hands, the death of Germany's hand-picked puppet king having made forcible conquest necessary. Serbia has been destroyed and the main artery of the new Empire, the great Berlin to Bagdad route, is completely under German control to within a few miles of the Orient city. William II. began this war as the ruler of 68 million souls. To-day he is the supreme war russia from 1815 to 1866, before Bismarck applied his policy of blood and iron. The Rhenish provinces of Saxony, and further Polish territory have been annexed.

&

lord of an empire of 176 millions, strategically located in the center of Europe. As Chéradame truly says: "This is the brutal, overwhelming fact which Americans must face if they wish to learn the sole solution of the war which will assure to them, as well as to the rest of the world, a durable peace."

Realizing the vast extent of her success, and fearful that further warfare may lead to its undoing, Germany is to-day frantically working for peace "on very moderate terms"; even, if necessary, "without annexations or indemnities." With the war beginning to go against her, she is generously willing to surrender (for the present) all the lands conquered from Russia, Roumania, France, and Belgium, and all of Servia save a narrow strip bordering the Berlin to Bagdad railway. She could restore all these and win the greatest victory in the history of Hohenzollern conquests. The blind would see only the *status quo ante.* Germany would see, and soon the rest of the world would see, the dream of a great Central European Germanic Empire come true (Figure 7). A real *status quo ante* is beyond the power of man to establish.

If there be those who, admitting the Hohenzollern policy of conquest up to and including the present war, nevertheless imagine that Germany would be willing to retire from the bloody struggle contented to let well enough alone provided her domination of Austria, Bulgaria, and Turkey were unimpaired, they should remember, in the first place, that the new and vastly stronger Germany would be ruled by the same Hohenzollern dynasty as before, imbued by the same passion for conquest which for more than five hundred years had been eminently successful, and never so much as in the present struggle. Let them give heed, in the second place, to the testimony of eminent Germans concerning their own ideas of Germany's future policy. Let them read von Bissing's memorandum to his government in which as Governor General of Belgium he boldly advocates the dethronement of the Belgian royal house and the forcible annexation of the country to Germany. Let them consider the sinister import of his candid declaration that reconciliation and peaceful domination are impossible, and that possession of Belgium is absolutely essential to the success of Germany's plans for future wars against England and France. Let them listen to the intellectual leaders of Germany: to Nietzsche teaching, "Ye shall love peace as a means to new wars,—and the short peace more than the long"; to Treitschke describing war as "an ordinance set by God" and "the most powerful maker of nations"; to Bernhardi declaring, "The lessons of history confirm the view that wars which have been deliberately provoked by far-seeing statesmen have had the happiest results"; and to Eucken asserting, "To us more than to any other nation is intrusted the true structure of human existence." Let them hear the revered pastors of Germany: Francke saying, "Germany is the representative of the highest morality, of the purest humanity, of the most chastened Christianity; its defeat would mean a falling back to the worst barbarism"; Lehman preaching, "The German soul is God's soul. It shall and will rule over mankind"; and König exhorting, "We must vanquish, because the downfall of Germanism would mean the downfall of humanity." Then perhaps will the thoughtless realize that the German nation, driven by a policy it cannot control, presses inevitably forward to new conquests, ever toward the goal of world dominion.

VI

TWO SIDES OF A SHIELD

WE have traced the history of the Prussian ideal of government to the present, and have found that its very existence depends upon an aggressive militarism which must ever conquer new dominions, or suffer decay and death. It follows that the American ideal of government must in the end conquer or be conquered. There is no truce in this warfare of ideals. Lincoln realized that the Union could not exist half slave and half free. The Hohenzollern realizes, and we must realize, that the world cannot exist half in political slavery and half in political freedom, half autocracy and half democracy.

It is fair to ask, however, whether after all the Prussian ideal of government may not be the best, if wisely administered. Human instinct may incline all mankind toward individual freedom, but instincts are not always safe guides to action. There is no *a priori* ground for assuming that the American ideal of government is superior to the Prussian ideal, and many an intelligent German has conscientiously argued that the Prussian Government is the most efficient, the most liberal, and the most truly free of all modern states. Let us in all candor consider whether the American ideal is so good or the Prussian ideal so bad that we should shed American blood to preserve the one and destroy the other.

No fair-minded man will deny that a government of the Prussian type may attain the highest efficiency in many fields of action. With an intelligent and

energetic ruler at the helm, with central-
ized control and responsibility, decisions
may be quickly reached and promptly
translated into action by the orderly
team work of a disciplined people.. For
more than five centuries the Hohenzollern dynasty has consistently and
efficiently progressed toward the ultimate
achievement of a single ideal, while more
liberal governments have blundered in
confusion through disastrous revolutions
and profound changes of national policy.
To-day Prussianized Germany, hope-
lessly outnumbered, holds the world at
bay, counting her military victories while
her enemies count their disastrous blun-
ders.   In social legislation, in municipal
government, Germany gives lessons to
the world.   In the application of science
to the arts and industries she has no equal.
Autocracy is admittedly efficient, democracy is certainly inefficient.

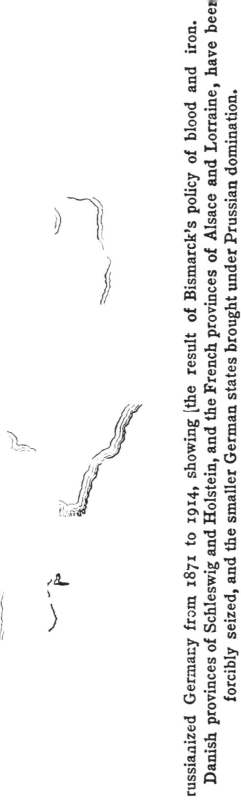

russianized Germany from 1871 to 1914, showing [the result of Bismarck's policy of blood and iron. Danish provinces of Schleswig and Holstein, and the French provinces of Alsace and Lorraine, have been forcibly seized, and the smaller German states brought under Prussian domination.

When every count in its favor has been
duly recorded, however, the truth remains
that the Prussian ideal of government is
so immoral, so iniquitous, so debasing
to the mind and the soul of man, that its
annihilation becomes the supreme duty
of the hour.   Let us review the indict-
ments against this monstrosity of the
Hohenzollern intellect.

In the first place it should be noted that
many of the beneficent features associated
with Prussian autocracy are not essen-
tially a part of the Prussian ideal of government.   They are, in not a few cases,
bribes offered to a discontented people to
quiet their grumblings against despotic
rule.   Take, for example, the work-
ingman's insurance laws to which Germans justly point with pride.   Both the
accident insurance law and the sickness
insurance law were introduced by Bismarck for the avowed purpose of quieting

the socialist agitation for greater political liberty, after drastic laws for the imprison-ment of socialist leaders had failed to crush their propaganda. A contented slave is better than one discontented, and it is a wise paternalism which provides for the material welfare of its subjects whether the form of government be good or bad. It has been well said that the German autocracy strives to govern so well that the people will have no desire to govern themselves.

The Prussian government of Germany is in point of fact a despotism in disguise. It has all the trappings of constitutional government, but the constitutional fea-tures are an empty sham designed to cloak the iron rule of Hohenzollern auto-cracy. If this seems an extreme state-ment, look for a moment at the structure of the Hohenzollern stronghold. Like our own government, there is a federation

of different states under a President, the
German Emperor. This President, like
our own, controls the foreign policy of the
federation and is commander-in-chief of
the army and navy. There is an upper
house or Senate called the Bundesrath,
and a lower House of Representatives,
the Reichstag. There is also a constitution defining the rights and privileges
of the people and their rulers. All this
sounds familiar to Americans, and might
easily deceive them, as it has deceived
many of the German people, into suppos-
ing that Germany enjoys self-government.
But let us look more closely. We find
that the upper house does not represent
the people, but consists (with three
exceptions) of men personally appoint-
ed by twenty-two hereditary German
princes. Even the lower house is not
truly representative, for the so-called
universal suffrage is a farce. The conser-

vative country districts, which are the strongholds of reactionary ideas, may have in proportion to their population ten times as much representation as the great cities where education and liberalism flourish. Less than two hundred thousand voters in certain country districts have sent to the Reichstag as many representatives as two million voters in some of the cities. In Prussia, the dominant German state, voting is based on a system which gives to the large taxpayers nearly thirty times as much representation as to the small taxpayers. Thus it is stated that in 1907 the large taxpayers, representing 3% of the voters, elected one-third of the electors, or as many as small taxpayers representing 87% of the voters.

Even this does not tell the whole story of autocratic Prussian rule. The Reichstag, or lower house, has no control over

. the Kaiser's salary or civil list, none over the Imperial Ministers who determine national and international policy, and almost none over legislation. Practically all legislation initiates with the upper house of monarchical appointees, and it may, with the Kaiser's consent, dissolve the lower house. The Kaiser has the power to declare defensive war, and since even this war of conquest is to him a defensive war, he may in practice declare war at will. He can make treaties, appoint or dismiss the chancellor and imperial ministers, and, with the consent of the upper house, dissolve the Reichstag. He is assigned enough votes in the upper house to enable him to pass any legislation which he desires, and to block any measure of which he disapproves. In a word, the Prince-appointed upper house controls the mis-representative lower house, and the Kaiser in turn controls both. Despite the outward form of constitutional government, Germany possesses the strongest autocratic despotism in the world to-day.

The Prussian government of Germany is an *absolute* despotism. The constitution is so skillfully devised as utterly to prevent any reform the Hohenzollern ruler does not approve, no matter how insistent the popular demand may be. The liberal-minded masses have a wholly inadequate representation in the Reichstag. But should reforms pass there, the monarchical appointees of the upper house, ever jealous of their prerogatives, stand ready to stifle them. And could we conceive that real reforms should win the support of a majority of these princely delegates, we must remember that fourteen votes are enough to defeat any amendment in this body, and that the Kaiser controls seventeen votes!   The despotic control is final and absolute.

The Prussian government of Germany is an *irresponsible* despotism.   The chief minister of the empire is the Imperial Chancellor, who is responsible to the Kaiser alone.   The Kaiser, in turn, owns responsibility only to God. William II., faithful to the centuries-old tradition of his Hohenzollern ancestors, seriously claims that he rules by the grace of God, and the claim is loyally supported by the conservative parties in the German state.   The hateful doctrine of the divine right of kings is a fundamental article of the Hohenzollern creed, although frequently disguised for the German people under the more subtle, and therefore more dangerous, doctrine of the divine right of the State.   Since the State is, in the last analysis, the Kaiser, the difference is one of words.   "We

Hohenzollerns," cries the present Kaiser, "take our crown from God alone, and to God alone are we responsible in the fulfillment of duty."

Prussianized Central Europe as it exists in the early part of 1917, showing the vast territory now complete the domination of Prussian militarism.

VII

THE DIVINE RIGHT OF THE STATE

OUT of evil things evil must come. No absolute and irresponsible despotism can breed peace, justice, and honor in the world. The evil may for a space be cloaked under the disguise of material prosperity, but the time soon comes when the horrid thing stands revealed in all its hideousness. We have seen that aggressive militarism is the inevitable accompaniment of the Prussian ideal of government. And militarism is an evil. It brutalizes mankind and substitutes the pagan doctrine that might makes right for the Christian doctrine that right is might. In the twinkling of

43

an eye the mask of material development which made Germany appear beautiful to the casual observer, drops to the ground, and we see all the hideousness of Prussian militarism exposed to the gaze of a surprised and indignant world. The indignation truly is justified, but not so the surprise; for the deeds of Prussian militarism are the logical and expectable consequences of the Prussian ideal of government.

The State is everything, the individual nothing. The State is a divine institution, and therefore can do no wrong. That which benefits the State is good, no matter what evil it may bring to individuals. Compared with the good of the State, the lives and the property of individuals, the suffering of mankind, and the harm done to other governments are as nothing. These are doctrines born of the Prussian ideal, and applied with conscientious consistency in the present war by the Prussian Government. "The State," writes Treitschke, "is the highest thing in the external society of man; above it there is nothing at all in the history of the world." The development of the State demands a policy of aggressive militarism, therefore war is moral and in the last analysis more to be desired than peace. The safety of the State demands expansion to the Mediterranean, hence the provocative ultimatum to Serbia was thoroughly justified. The advantage of the State necessitates a quick attack on France through neutral Belgium, therefore the wholesale slaughter of an innocent people while unfortunate is a wholly proper measure. The security of the army, the strong right arm of the State, is promoted by terrorizing the civilian populations of occupied territories, and so the shooting of hostages, the burning of cities, and the commission of unspeakable outrages are to be tolerated for the good end they serve. International law forbids the levying of indemnities on captured cities, the deportation of civilians, the employment of enemy subjects in military work, the bombardment of open towns; but the State is higher than international law and these things may be done if they are of advantage to the State. Humanity forbids the slaughter of non-combatants and the murder of women and children; but the State is higher than humanitarian considerations and these crimes are defensible if they are of convenience to the State. To the logical believer in the Prussian ideal of government, "military necessity" is an all-sufficient explanation for any crime, no matter how barbarous or revolting. There is no crime, if the State—that is, the Hohenzollern autocrat—gains some advantage from the deed.

We need not deal specifically with the burning of Louvain, the bombardment of Rheims cathedral, the Zeppelin raids on Paris and London, the sinking of the *Lusitania* and other submarine atrocities, the deportation of girls from Lille and of workmen from Belgium, the judicial murder of Edith Cavell and Capt. Fryatt, because all of these are but symptoms, and perfectly logical and normal symptoms, of the aggressive militarism which is inextricably bound up with the Prussian ideal of government. A people devoted to the Prussian ideal become insensible to wrongs which revolt the consciences of other peoples, not because such a people is inherently more barbarous, but because militarism and the false doctrine of the divine right of the State inevitably degrade the ideals and brutalize the instincts of any political society. The American people, submissive for a few centuries to the false teachings of the Prussian ideal, imbued with the pernicious idea that they were destined by God to force the superior culture of their divine State upon the rest of the world for its own good, would commit acts as barbarous as any which have stained the record of German warfare.

VIII

THE ISSUE

WE have seen that the Prussian ideal of government and the American ideal cannot exist together in the world, and that the Prussian ideal is of necessity vicious in its nature and degrading in its effects. For Americans there is but one issue from this dilemma. The Prussian ideal must perish, the American ideal must ·live. We fight not to avenge the *Lusitania*, not to rebuild Louvain, not to exact reparation for murdered women and children. We fight to slay the government which taught its people to commit such damnable atrocities. We fight that never again may a great nation with cynical insolence throw in the face of the world the base assertions that treaties are scraps of paper, that necessity knows no law, that might is the right of the strongest, and that the State can do no wrong. We fight to hurl the Hohenzollern and his dangerous doctrine of divine right upon the scrap-heap of useless trumpery, and to set the German people in his place, that they may learn to rule themselves.

How shall the end be achieved? Not by a half-way war, not by conciliation or compromise. Great ends are not achieved by petty measures. The Imperial German armies must be defeated on the battlefield and driven from the lands they conquered. The German people must learn that for all its inefficiency, democracy is stronger than disciplined autocracy. Restitution of the fruits of past conquest must be required, Bosnia and Herzegovina, Alsace-Lorraine and Po-

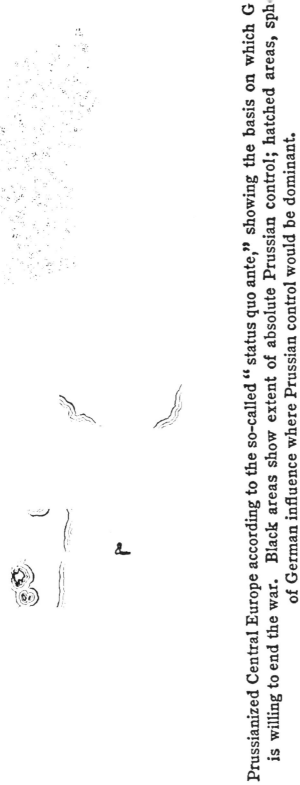

Prussianized Central Europe according to the so-called " status quo ante," showing the basis on which G
is willing to end the war. Black areas show extent of absolute Prussian control; hatched areas, sph
of German influence where Prussian control would be dominant.

land restored to rightful sovereignty. The German people must learn that the dream of a Central European Empire, founded on military conquest, is forever dashed to earth. Reparation for grievous wrongs, so far as these may be repaired by money indemnities, must be exacted. The German people must learn that upon the guilty aggressor, not upon the innocent victim, falls the heavy burden of restoring ravished lands, rehabilitating burned and pillaged cities, supporting ruined homes, and indemnifying those whose innocent loved ones were foully wronged or slain. War in the past has been immensely profitable to Germany. She must be taught that it is the most costly crime a nation can commit. With these ends achieved we may reasonably hope that the German people, sick of the bloody disasters born of Prussian militarism, will awaken from the trance in which they live and throw off the hateful Hohenzollern yoke. If they do not, then we must fight to force the central citadel of Prussian power. We must not lay down the sword till the Hohenzollern throne is empty.

When the sufferings of this war press heavily upon us, when long casualty lists fill the columns of our papers, when business losses mount high and the people clamor for bread, there will arise a loud and insistent demand for an inconclusive peace. Then let us envisage the magnitude of the issue of this war, and prepare to make sacrifices commensurable to the ends we seek. Let us remember that we fight to tear out, root and branch, an ideal of government deep-grown in central Europe. The gathered strength of centuries is not overcome by the efforts of a day, nor the struggles of a deluded people stilled without much suffering.

The contest may lengthen into years, defeats may humiliate us and dangers increase, every family may mourn its dead and every heart be heavy with foreboding; still let us fight on, shoulder to shoulder with our gallant allies, till the liberty of the world be won. As Christ died to make men holy, let us die to make men free; for God *is* marching on.

The War and Humanity"

By
James M. Beck

Notable Sequel to "The Evidence in the Case"

Mr. Beck's volume was a classic the moment it ap-
·cd.   We know of no more logical and lucid discussion
he essential facts and problems of the great war, nor
more truly, consistently, and even vigorously Amer-
in its spirit.   We should be well content to let it
d, if there were no other, as the authentic expres-
of the highest aspirations, the broadest and most
:trating vision, and the most profound convictions of
American nation on matters which have never been
assed and have only twice been rivalled in vital in-
sts in all our history."—*New York Tribune.*

:ODORE ROOSEVELT'S OPINION

It is the kind of a book, which every self-respecting.
:rican, who loves his country, should read."

Revised and Enlarged Edition
:arly 400 pages. $1.50 net.   By mail, $1.60

At All Booksellers

G. P. Putnam's Sons

The Eviden
the Cas

A Discussion of the Moral Responsibili
1914, as Disclosed by the Diplom
of England, Germany, Russia,
Austria, and Belgium

By
JAMES M. BECK, I
Late Assistant Attorney-General (

With an Introduction
The Hon. JOSEPH H. (
Late U. S. Ambassador to Grea

11th Printing—Revised Edition with
Material
12°.   Over 280 pages. $1.25 net.

"Mr. Beck's book is so extrem
from beginning to end that it is
once begun to lay it down and
reading, and we are not surprise
only that it has had an immense s
and America, but that its transl
languages of the other nations
been demanded."—*Hon. Joseph
The New York Times.*

New York   **G. P. Putnam's So**

CPSIA information can be obtained
at www.ICGtesting.com
Printed in the USA
BVHW042317290119
539019BV00010B/192/P